TONY WARREN'S SKETCH

'Falmouth-born Painter of Ships & th

Compiled and written by Sheila Bird

© Sheila Bird 1998

ISBN 0 9512236 5 8

Bird of Freedom,
The Shrubbery,
17 Grovehill Drive,
Falmouth,
Cornwall, TR11 3HS.

Tony Warren (1930 – 1994)

As far as many people are concerned, Falmouth has not been the same since Tony left us, for he was an institution in himself, and a great ambassador for Falmouth. In a profession with more than its fair share of posers, he was like a breath of fresh air; he was the real thing. He was born into a family steeped in salty tradition, and lived out his life on the Falmouth waterfront, where he was much influenced by his boyhood experiences during the Second World War. His distinctive sketches and paintings reflect all this, with feeling and charm.

As well as being a place of work, Tony's harbourside studio served as a sounding-board for the waterfront fraternity, and was a welcome port of call for locals and visitors, who felt privileged to be accepted into his world. He heightened people's awareness of the past, and was able to unite the past with the present. He breathed life into history, and enriched the lives of others with his conversational and artistic skills. As a writer and old friend of Tony's, I was pleased to be invited to compile this book by the Warren family, and in doing so, I hope that Tony's creativity will live on and continue to delight people for many years to come.

Sheila Bird, Falmouth, 1998

4

Flushing as seen from the quay at Greenbank

The evocative sight of packet ship posters on the bar room walls of the historic Greenbank Hotel set Tony musing one sunny summer's evening in the early 1980s. 'The old Falmouth Packet Ships, you know; the little two masted brigs, used to be here around 1688 'till about 1840. During that period 'twas all Falmouth Packets. It did really *make* Falmouth. It made Flushing, over there. See, Flushing was built by Dutch engineers about 1616. O' course, Falmouth was such a rough old place in that period. The genteel lot lived over there. See, there's Admiral Pellew's house over there, where Nelson called one time. Oh, yes. They wouldn't have riff-raff over there – as they had over 'ere. Only the ones that *lived* there and *worked* there were *permitted there*.'

Tony Warren

One of the famous old *Packet* ships, which brought prestige and prosperity to Falmouth. For the establishment of the *Post Office Packet Station* in 1688 gave rise to Falmouth's *Golden Age*. A special fleet of fast vessels rigged as brigs, with two masts carrying square sails, a long bowsprit, headsails and a large gaff mizzen-sail was constructed locally. Their carrying of valuable cargoes attracted the attentions of pirates and other villains of the sea, and these men of the *Packet Service* have been acknowledged for their bravery in the seafaring story of our nation. One exploit, which captures the romantic imagination concerns John Bull, whose ship, the *Marlborough*, was set upon by a French Privateer in 1810 as she was about to enter Falmouth Harbour. However, after a very spirited skirmish, during which the Privateer received two broadsides, the Frenchmen decided that discretion was the better part of valour, and limped off.

The loss of the *Packet Service* to Southampton in the mid-19th Century was a severe blow for Falmouth, which then turned its attentions to the establishment of the Docks.

'Falmouth for Orders'

The *Scottish Moors*, constructed at Stockton in 1890, entering Falmouth Harbour in 1901. She later sailed under the Norwegian flag as the *Svaland*, and was a merchant trading vessel.

Ships like this were colloquially known as *windjammers*. But if this slang term, coined at a time of rivalry between the crews of steam ships and sailing ships was originally intended to be somewhat derisory, it came to evoke the rollicking, romantic spirit of the great days of sail for poets and dreamers.

Falmouth Quay Punt

The sea was the lifeblood of Falmouth, with its capacious natural harbour, and its advantageous *first-in-last-out* situation in regard to the English Channel. As the 19th-Century scene of multifarious maritime activity, where ocean-going skippers called to receive orders in respect of cargo movements, the sturdy, speedy and dependable Falmouth Quay punts evolved to meet the lucrative ship-to-shore trade and the everyday needs of the busy Cornish port.

Their short, stumpy masts were designed to enable the little vessels to sail under the yard arms of the great sailing ships to allow them to get alongside.

The Oyster Boat *Zona* rounding St Just Buoy in Falmouth Harbour. Having been constructed in Mevagissey as a trawler and long-liner, she has proved to be readily adaptable, and has thus become well known on the Falmouth scene as an oyster-dredger.

Although oyster-dredging has been carried out since Roman times, and possibly earlier, there was renewed activity in the mid-19th Century, with lucrative local spin-offs, as this *West Briton* report of March 1844 testifies:

Owing to a scarcity in the eastern grounds (the Thames estuary), the oyster has swelled into importance in Falmouth harbour, and attracted the attention, not alone of fishermen, but of shoemakers, carpenters, masons, and even labourers in agriculture, who now drop their usual implements, and ply the oar, and the dredge, to bring (these shellfish) to day light. From 150 to 200 boats may now be seen on a fine day dotted over the surface of the harbour, engaged in this fishery. From the scarcity to the eastward, the price given is great, and all the fishermen and others engaged in it derive handsome wages, and are indeed making little fortunes. It may be calculated that not less than seven thousand pounds worth of oysters will be exported from Falmouth harbour this season.

However, things were not so good in the 1980s and 1990s, when the industry was hit by an oyster disease and pollution problems.

A busy harbour scene, drawn from Greenbank Quay, with the dockyard cranes, Falmouth Hotel and the church in the background, and the Royal Cornwall Yacht Club and two working boats in the foreground.

The *Waterwitch* in Falmouth in 1930

This grand old timer was destined to become the last cargo-carrying British square-rigger to be seen around our shores, and as such provided the opportunity for young steamship officers wishing to become Trinity House pilots, to gain the required experience.

The *Waterwitch* was constructed in Poole in 1871 as a wooden brig, supposedly from the timbers of an old frigate. She was originally Portsmouth-owned, and underwent extensive repairs in 1877 before being converted into a brigantine seven years later.

Having come under Cornish ownership, it seemed likely that she would end her days as a wreck in Newlyn Harbour. However, she was acquired by Edward Stephens of Fowey, who had her transformed into a beautiful barquentine to enhance his existing fleet.

After the First World War Captain Charles Henry Deacon (a swarthy, kindly, God-fearing Devonian, who wore golden earrings), took command of her, and she plied the china-clay trade all around the coast before being taken out of service in 1936, and languishing at Par. But the Estonians reckoned there was life in the Old Girl yet, and they were right. For she enjoyed a period of somewhat obscure rejuvenation around the Baltic ports.

The old Falmouth *Pilot Cutter No. 13*, meeting a clipper ship off the Lizard in 1898. The *Falmouth Pilot Boat Association* was established in 1887, to bring together all the pilots operating in family boats under the authority of *Trinity House*.

These stylish pilot boats, described in 1907 as 'smart little cutters with lines like a racer, which could sail within two points of the wind, and ride out a gale without shipping a sea,' were designed for speed. For there had always been fierce competition to be first on the scene to secure the contract for pilotage. The hazards of these waters were notorious the world over, and the crewmen of many an incoming vessel must have felt elated to see a pilot boat looming up out of the mist, and bearing down upon them. This would be followed by an exchange of signals and brief communication through a speaking trumpet to establish where she was from, where she was bound, and the nature of her cargo.

The pilot was transferred to the ship by means of a small punt or skiff, launched through a door in the gunwale. Once the pilot left the ship, which might be in Fowey, Plymouth or further afield, it was up to him to find his own way home, often on foot.

The *Lady Daphne*

There was great excitement on the Falmouth waterfront in July 1984, when the former Rochester ketch-barge *Lady Daphne* was seen in the harbour, acting as 'mother ship' for the Drake Fellowship's shrimpers during the regatta. Tony recalled her adventures surrounding the Boxing Day of 1927, when she was caught in freshening north-westerly weather erupting into blizzards, whilst on passage from the Thames to Plymouth with a cargo of bricks and tiles. Having been unable to gain entry to Plymouth Sound, the Master was lost overboard, and she careered on down the Channel as the remaining two men frantically ignited flares and tried to attract attention. Her plight was noticed by the Lizard lifeboatmen, who put to sea and gallantly rescued them after a 12 mile chase, leaving the *Lady Daphne* to her own devices.

With wheel set, she hammered on, maintaining a steady course, and was spotted next morning tacking through Crow Sound in classical style. Anticipating an equally skilful rounding off to anchor, the onlookers winced as she centred on and ran aground on Tresco. Tony particularly relished the ending of this colourful tale, whereby the lifeboatmen who had gone to her aid were astonished to find her deserted, except for a lonely canary, 'singing merrily in his cage.'

Falmouth Working Boats Racing in the Harbour

Tony's father, who like his father before him worked in Falmouth Docks and went to sea in the lean times, always maintained harbour surveillance from his High Street home in his leisure moments.

'My father sat, most of his evenings (except when he went out to the pub), in an old armchair by the window, with his binoculars, smoking a pipe. Took in everything. Everything that moved, 'e saw. And 'e had this home made sort o' shelf by the window, so there was means o' tapping out his pipe.'

Peter Warren particularly enjoyed the spectacle of the working boats racing. For the general love of the sea was such that those who gleaned a livelihood from oyster-dredging and allied maritime activity, took to their boats for recreational purposes. These traditions continue today, and although speedier and more sophisticated craft may have appeared on the scene, there remains a very special regard for these handsome and pleasing old working boats.

A walker on the Cornish cliffs, who was moved by the sight of a magnificent ship in full sail at the beginning of the 20th Century wrote:

And then slowly round the Lizard Head came a large white full-rigged ship with every sail set. A phantom ship she seemed to be, from some distant land of dreams, so stately, so shapely, so apparently motionless she lay, carved like a cameo against the golden haze of the horizon. Above her towered an immense cumulous cloud – also divinely white – piercing the blue heaven like some mighty alp. And ship and cloud were as a poet's dream .....

For those who love ships and the sea, the relatively recently established tradition of the Tall Ships Race allows us to savour such spectacles, and reflect on our proud maritime heritage.

The 3-masted Topsail Schooner *Sir Winston Churchill* was the first ship built by the Sail Training Association (STA), for the express purpose of offering young people the character-building opportunity of training under sail. She was built in Yorkshire in 1966 and was joined by her Scottish-built sister ship *Malcolm Miller* two years later.

The British Barquentine *Royalist*, constructed in 1971 and owned by the Sea Cadets Association, is a familiar sight in Weymouth, Falmouth and other southern ports as well as taking part in the Tall Ships Races. She was a particular favourite of Tony's.

The stately Norwegian square rigger *Christian Radich* entering Falmouth Harbour in 1988. This vessel, constructed in 1937 played a traditional role before becoming a veteran of the Tall Ships scene. The uplifting sight of the Tall Ships around our shores arouses an awareness of our maritime past and present. For as the poet said:

> *They mark our passage as a race of men;*
> *Earth will not see such ships as this agen.*

The *TSS Princess Victoria* was one of a number of pleasure boats seen around Falmouth Harbour in the first part of the 20th Century, providing a regular service for the rural communities around the waterways, as well as catering for holidaymakers, who could purchase tickets for circular trips in conjunction with Great Western Railways. Her twin screw design, countering any loss of draught, made her particularly suitable for river, rather than seafaring excursions.

This handsome vessel followed in the wake of two previous towing and passenger-carrying steamers named *Victoria*, which had been constructed for the *Fal Steamship Company* by *Cox & Company* in 1900 and 1901, and been sold out of the area. By the time she was completed in 1907, the *Fal Steamship Company* had amalgamated with *Benney & Company* of Truro, to become the *River Fal Steamship Company Limited*. Thus when she first came on the scene, it was diplomatically in the white livery of her predecessors, but sporting the distinctive tri-coloured funnel of the *Benneys*. She was subsequently repainted in grey, with black gunwales.

The *Princess Victoria*, like some of her contemporaries, was requisitioned by the Admiralty in 1942, and never returned to her home waters.

The Steam Tug *St Mawes*, formerly the *Arusha*

Traditional harbour tugs might be defined as small, powerful vessels, used for towing others, and for manoeuvring large ships in and out of their berths. Some were capable of 'outside' and salvage work. They evolved locally as steam-powered towage vessels with a passenger-carrying capacity, and were regarded by Tony as the workhorses of Falmouth Harbour.

In 1959 the Falmouth fleet was renamed after the Cornish saints, and as time went by steam tugs were ousted by the more efficient diesel variety. Thus the *St Mawes* was last seen being towed out of the harbour by the tug *Olivierssen* on 17 January 1984, en route for *Oosterschelde*. The *St Merryn* was taken out of service at the same time.

The Falmouth Steam Tug *St Denys*, constructed by a Scottish shipyard for the *Falmouth Towage Company* as the *Northgate Scot* in 1929, spent all her working life in the port. She was acquired by *Falmouth Maritime Museum* in 1981, when her next port of call was scheduled to be the scrapyard, but she was subsequently sold to the French, to become a floating exhibit in Douarnenez.

There has always been a bond between Cornwall and Brittany, and Tony relished his colourful adventures, centred around Douarnenez's Maritime Festival.

Tony's childhood interpretation of a *Sunderland*

Sunderland Flying Boats could be seen around the Port of Falmouth in the period leading up to the Second World War, when small boys were thrilled to witness their take-offs along Carrick Roads, and their descents, when they would land on the surface of the water and taxi around before taking up their moorings between Trefusis Point and Flushing.

The *Sunderland Flying Boats*, based in Plymouth Sound, were prompt to zoom into action when war was declared on September 3rd, 1939, for the following dawn saw them making their first of hundreds of anti-submarine patrols in the Western Approaches. They had the remarkable ability to fight off numbers of more manoeuvrable, better armed attackers. They were subsequently equipped with extra machine guns to respond to deck gunners; a situation which earned them the nickname *Flying Porcupines!*

A dramatic scene from Tony's childhood imagination, with all guns blazing

Naval Motor Torpedo Boats (*MTBs*), *Motor Gun Boats* (*MGBs*) and the RAF's *High Speed Launches* (*HSLs*), were familiar in these wartime waters.

The concept of planing craft, designed to lift and reduce their draught in the water dates back to 1872. Research into achieving higher speeds intensified in the early part of the 20th Century, stimulated by the desires of the well-heeled racing fraternity. The knowledge thus gained was utilised in the construction of *Coastal Motor Boats* (*CMBs*), in the First World War, which subsequently developed a torpedo-carrying and mine-laying capacity.

Further work on *MTBs* in the 1930s demonstrated that torpedoes could be mounted in such a way as to achieve a bow discharge. Initially the idea was to have a single torpedo tube above the mess deck, with a firing range through the stem of the boat, while a second torpedo could be carried on the after-deck. Re-loading could be achieved from the rear end of the torpedo tube, which was straddled by the helmsman's seat on the open bridge. This undoubtedly created quite a sensation when the torpedo was fired. However, difficulties and delay in re-loading, particularly in rough weather, led to on-going adaptations. Their speed and manoeuvrability allowed them to creep up on targets, such as submarines, and let fly with their torpedoes. But those who put to sea in such craft were very vulnerable, and indeed, only two of the twenty-two sub-lieutenants who signed up for *MTBs* in 1939 lived to see the end of the war.

Robert Hichens, our much decorated, famous local hero, who was brought up in Flushing and loved sailing in the harbour, had great qualities of leadership and tactical ingenuity. His unfinished book *We Fought Them in Gunboats*, published in 1944, did not tell the full story, for he was killed by a stray shell in 1943, before he had fully played out the drama.

Sir Lancelot of 1940

A. WARREN
Nov : 1944

A witty interpretation of *Sir Lancelot of 1940 – by Antonio de Falmouth*, at the age of fourteen.

The Methodist Church on the Moor was bombed twice in the early part of the war, when Falmouth Harbour was a prime target. This sketch is drawn from Tony's boyhood recollection of the scene witnessed on his way to school the following morning.

'Commandos exercising on the Moor at Falmouth, on a Sunday morning, 1942, smoke grenades all round! On the tree the little yellow patch was painted on many places, in gas detecting paint – if it changed colour there was gas present,' explained Tony.

Trevethan Infants School, where Tony began his education, was badly damaged during a nocturnal raid of May 1941. The school, situated off Webber Street, never re-opened, but it later saw service as the H.Q. of 1157 Squadron of the Air Training Corps.

The return from St Nazaire after the daring raid on the heavily defended, Nazi occupied port, in a mission code-named *Operation Chariot*. Few civilians had been aware of the departure of an odd assortment of vessels, which had gathered in Falmouth Bay, in March 1942. Things were similarly kept very low key as they straggled home, one after another, having accomplished what many regard as 'the greatest raid of all,' thereby thwarting Hitler's plans to strengthen his position in the North Atlantic. Despite being forbidden by his father to go near the Prince of Wales Pier, young Tony had the shocking experience of seeing the *MLs* returning; their open decks strewn with dead and wounded commandos, and the corpses being landed on the quay. In all 168 brave men lost their lives, while numbers of others had been wounded or taken to prisoner of war camps.

An evening strafing of the docks by an *FW 190* with extended fuel tanks, around 1942/3.

During his boyhood, Tony witnessed a number of incidents like this. 'They came from airfields like St Brieuc and all along the coast of Brittany and the Channel Islands,' he said. 'They came in singly and in pairs. As a child you could identify them all, naturally. We used to make models of them. We thought they were the greatest things.'

May Morning, Falmouth, 1944

Tony's intensely personal, graphic portrayal of the build up to D-Day, as witnessed from the Falmouth waterfront, is full of feeling and exudes the spirit of the times.

'Everybody knew that something was coming up,' said Tony. 'There was nothing but vehicles, men and equipment being brought in. Bloody great bulks o' gear wherever you went, and landing craft all over the place. You couldn't believe it! Then suddenly you'd see the harbour clear, and everybody thought, '*This is it! It's on!*' Then next morning they'd be back again. This happened two or three times. Then suddenly they went – the same as that! And that was it! After that there was no fuss, and everything went strangely quiet.'

Tony's wholehearted relationship with the Falmouth waterfront and the vivid experiences of childhood remained with him throughout his life. Thus no warship could ever enter harbour without being captured by him – in pen and ink.

F52

A flotilla of warships arriving in Falmouth Harbour on exercise in June, 1989.

Tony Warren   Falmouth
19 June 1989

The *Arun Class* lifeboat *Elizabeth Ann*, which came on station on 8 June, 1979. At her naming ceremony Vivian Pentecost took over as Coxswain from Arthur 'Toby' West. 'There is a tradition in Falmouth that the outgoing Coxswain takes the boat out, and the incoming Coxswain brings her in,' explained Viv Pentecost, who was subsequently succeeded by John Barton and Alan Barnes.

Padstow's 47 ft *Tyne Class* Lifeboat *James Burrough* cutting a dash

Lifeboatmen from all over the country always relished their visits to Falmouth, and the opportunity to have a yarn with Tony. He was a great friend to the RNLI. He was a tireless fundraiser and donated countless paintings for raffle prizes.

Before becoming a professional artist, Tony worked as a signwriter with leading local builder E. H. Moss. Having acquired the highly specialised skill of gilding, Tony's talents were much in demand. 'We used to do all the signs for the Woolworth's shops in Cornwall,' he explained. 'Twenty three carat gold; gold leaf. 'Twas a technique; a difficult technique. And in the end I finished up doing all the lifeboats in Cornwall when they came in for refits at the Little Falmouth Boatyard over at Flushing.'

The *SS Uganda* was constructed by *Barclay, Curle & Company* of Glasgow for the *British India Line* in 1952, and operated all over the East, the Far East, India, Burma, East and South Africa and Australia. She was converted into an educational cruise ship in Holland in 1968, and went to war in the Falklands as a hospital ship. At one point when she was employed as a troopship in the South Atlantic, she clocked up 500 days without docking at any one port.

In the mid 1980s the *SS Uganda Society* was formed with the aim of preserving her, as the last of a shipping line which once had the greatest single fleet in the world. But sadly this was not to be. Having been laid up in King Harry Reach of the Fal for several months, the *Uganda* was sold to a Taiwanese ship-breaking company, and the once grand Old Lady, now rusty and tarnished, left the port in May 1986 in a blaze of glory. She left as the *Triton*, sailing under the flag of *St Vincent and the Grenadines*. But if this symbol of our former maritime prestige was forced to leave our shores for the last time, this voyage was destined to find a place in our colourful seafaring history. For she was beset by thieves at Port Said and by pirates in the Suez Canal, encountered problems with rain and heat in the Red Sea, experienced boiler troubles in the Gulf of Aden and was threatened by typhoons in the South China Sea. When they arrived off Kaohsiung 55 days later, all the breaking berths were occupied, so she was spared the indignity of being run into the breakers yard alongside the remains of other vessels, for the time being .....

Captain J. D. Coxe, who had taken her on her last voyage described how a month later, still at anchor, she was caught by typhoon Wayne, and drove ashore. She was left at an angle of 70 degrees on her starboard side, with her keel facing shorewards and her propeller sticking up in the air. In this submissive, yet provocative pose, she was cocking a snook at the breakers yard, while demonstrating a willingness to yield to the natural elements.

62

H.M.Y. BRITANNIA
AT SEA
9th June, 1985

Dear Mr Warren

Queen Elizabeth The Queen Mother bids me write and thank you so much for your gift.

Queen Elizabeth was very touched by your kind thought in presenting Her Majesty with such a delightful watercolour of BRITANNIA entering Falmouth Harbour. Your painting will indeed always remind Her Majesty of a very enjoyable visit to Cornwall.

The Queen Mother sends you her warmest good wishes for the years ahead.

Comptroller to
Queen Elizabeth The Queen Mother

Tony Warren, Esq.,

Flying the Flag for Britain

The royal yacht *Britannia* made several notable visits to Falmouth, and was a familiar sight in local waters. Indeed, walkers on the cliffs sometimes saw her poised off the Helford to allow her captain to be whisked ashore to his riverside home. A posting aboard the *Britannia* was always regarded as the most glamorous of opportunities in the Royal Navy.

This splendid ship, constructed at *John Brown's Shipyard* on the *Clyde*, and launched in April 1953, was noted for her uncluttered, elegant design and was the envy of the world. There was great sadness when she was decommissioned in 1997.

Tony's sensitive and charming portrayal of North Quay and the Custom House basin in the 1890s, captures the spirit of the times, when the work-a-day maritime scene was filled with dignity and beauty, in harmony with Nature.

The environment of Custom House basin a century later, demonstrates the evolutionary process in a setting which has managed to retain its identity and charm. Sail gave way to funnel, and steam to diesel, as some long-standing traditions were re-aligned. Thus the old steam tug *St Denys*, seen here, became a museum exhibit, before being acquired by the French as a period piece.

Tony's bold yet delicate scraperboard technique breathes life and atmosphere into the view towards the Greenbank from Laundry Quay, now styled 'the Packet Quays'.

Penryn's present parish church, pleasingly described in 1865 as 'the pretty church of St Gluvias, embosomed in trees,' has longstanding salty associations, and its atmospheric churchyard has provided the last resting place for many victims of shipwreck.

St Budock Church

A religious community was known to exist in this vicinity in the 6th Century, perhaps on this site. The anciently established churches of St Budock and St Gluvius were closely associated in early times, and both served as mother churches for the area.

The distinctive tower of Falmouth's parish church of King Charles the Martyr dominates the maritime scene. One of Cornwall's worst shipwrecks occurred in this harbour of refuge in January 1814, when the transport *Queen* was driven ashore on Trefusis Point during a violent blizzard. Most of the 195 victims were buried at St Gluvias, Budock and Mylor.

Penwerris Church, where Tony was married. This architecturally pleasing church of St Michael & All Angels, was constructed in 1827 on a site donated by the Bassets of Tehidy, who had made a fortune out of mining. It served the higher seafaring echelons of society, who occupied prestigious houses overlooking the harbour and Flushing's quaint quayside.

Mawnan Smith Church

A heavenly aura surrounds this isolated, pleasingly proportioned little church in its romantic sylvan setting on the clifftop at the mouth of the Helford River, in an area well known to smugglers of old.

Other books by Sheila Bird

* Bygone Falmouth
* County Companion: Dorset
* Lyme Regis, Uplyme & Charmouth Companion
* Bygone Truro
* Seaton, Axmouth, Colyton, Colyford, Beer & Branscombe Companion
* The Book of Somerset Villages
* Bygone Penzance & Newlyn
* Sidmouth, Budleigh Salterton & District Companion
* Exmouth, The Exe Estuary & Dawlish Companion
* Around the Waterways of the Fal
* The Book of Cornish Villages
* Cornish Curiosities
* Mayday! Preserving Life from Shipwreck off Cornwall
* Tales of Old Cornwall
* The Mevagissey Companion
* Cornish Sea Stories
* Bodmin Moor

Creeds the Printers, Broadoak, Bridport, Dorset DT6 5NL (01308) 423411